uld

t. y

r I

uever is
mportant to
d against all
l m

washingtonpublishing.net

Nicole McLaren Campbell

Make it Count

WASHINGTON **PUBLISHING**

Published by Washington Publishing
Washington, DC, USA

Why?

I wrote this short e-book simply because a security guard at Television Jamaica, a local television station in Jamaica, asked me to do so, after an appearance I made on a morning talk show. She said that she felt inspired by me, but wished she had something she could sit with, read and use when she needed encouragement. By sharing personal stories and examples of how I work through obstacles in my life, I hope to show you that you can do the same. From this book I want you to see, or be reminded (in the same way I have) that successful people aren't born that way, and with the right toolkit we can all do what successful people do, and find our own success. I've long felt the calling to become an author, and I see myself reaching millions of people through text. Writing a book has felt, and still feels, so intimidating ... so I started the way I recommend you start on a goal that feels too huge - with a first step. Welcome to my first ebook – a short set of tips in 5 key areas – the 5 areas are ones that I believe must be mastered if you hope to unlock your vision and maximize your potential: Fear, Having the Courage to Ask for What You Want, Procrastination, Tuning into Your Purpose and Staying Motivated. By showing you how I keep moving in spite of, and often beyond, the most common obstacles that lead us to stand in our own way, I hope that you feel empowered to keep moving!

Chapter 1

Fear

How to get over fear is one of the most common questions I am asked. It is a natural emotion and experiencing fear is part of what it means to be human. I have experienced fear, and still do, every time I decide to step out into unchartered territory, to take a risk, dream a bigger dream or ask a question I am not sure of the answer to. I can't remember experiencing fear until I was about 13 ... when I was part of an online summit organized by the Massachusetts Institute of Technology and was announced as the winner prematurely by my high school. I remember being terrified of not actually winning – I was afraid of what others would say or think and I was afraid of being embarrassed. I did end up winning, but, somehow the fear of not accomplishing my big dreams and goals has never really left me since then. Still, I kept acting. When I was 15 I decided to apply to competitive private college prep boarding school, Phillips Academy, to seek greater challenge academically. The stakes were pretty low - no one knew I was even applying, my parents didn't want me to leave Jamaica and I wasn't 100% sure I wanted to leave Jamaica either - so, I wasn't afraid of not getting in. However, when the courses were harder than I could have imagined, and the homesickness was like a heavy, thick blanket all around me, I became completely terrified of failure. With the college application process upon me almost as soon as I set foot on Andover's campus, I feared not getting into a prestigious university – a dream that I had for myself for as long as I could remember, and what I knew so many friends and family expected of me. I feared not measuring up to the awesome talent I was surrounded by, inside and outside of the classroom. I questioned my worth as my safe identity as academic superstar, one nurtured and reinforced over my years in high school in Jamaica, came under threat. I didn't know the answers to the questions the teachers asked. I read, and re-read, the textbooks but just couldn't seem to grasp the concepts as quickly as I was accustomed to.

Three months and many tears after arriving on campus, I was on the brink of giving up and returning to Jamaica. I prayed and prayed to God and felt deeply that I needed to dig deep, that somehow my ability to overcome and succeed at Andover would have far-reaching implications for my life. So I listened to Him, I tried to block the fear out, and focus on what I needed to do to be successful in this more challenging environment. What took others 3 hours to complete took me 6, but I did it anyway - with 100% of what I had to give! I decided I would need to focus on what I had, not what I didn't have. I knew that I needed to stop comparing myself to others, and wondering why I couldn't have the talent in Math another student seemed to have or the athletic prowess of another. I had to trust that I had unique gifts to offer the world, even if I wasn't exactly sure of what those gifts were. After coming perilously close to throwing in the towel, I boldy applied to Princeton University Early Decision. I recognized, and acknowledged my fear of not being admitted, a fear that was not helped by a college counselor who thought I was aiming way too high. I focused on success – I prayed, I visualized myself at Princeton, I prayed more, then filled out the application with the best expectations and full conviction. When I got in, I really understood the power of moving beyond fear, tuning out what others say about one's possibilities and got a glimpse of what NOT pursuing my dreams could mean for my life.

What I've also learned though, is that if one does not continue to push against fear, even after major life lessons like what I learned at Andover, fear can creep back in our subconscious and limit action and possibility. I know this because when I landed at Princeton I slowly but surely, again, became unsure of my place, intimidated by others I thought belonged more, who were more talented than I could ever hope to be. I didn't go after opportunities; I just worked hard in my classes but didn't do much more.

Ironically, my first encounter with real disappointment and failure – applying to the London School of Economics and not getting in, gave me the freedom I needed to find my fearlessness. How? Well, I failed and I didn't die, I got over it, and focused on the opportunities at the smaller, lesser-known School of Advanced Study at the University of London. In the short year (or less) it took me to get my Masters, I applied and received extra scholarships and jobs with the Commonwealth Institute and opened myself up to new experiences. How ironic that failure freed me from the fear of it.

I returned to Jamaica open to possibility, not one hundred percent sure of how I would build the life of my dreams but pretty sure that I was going to do it somehow. That belief fueled my work at the Ministry of Education for the year I spent there, and for sure, my ability to embrace risk and expose myself to failure gave me the courage I needed to resign from that job when I wanted to start a business in educational consulting. Of course, the support and encouragement of my then boyfriend now husband, and my family (especially my mom and sister) had a great impact as well.

My fears have never disappeared, and sometimes I feel them so deeply I fret, cry and meltdown, but, I take the action anyway. I cried on my way to my first speaking engagement. I expose myself to hurt, embarrassment and failure repeatedly, and the more I do it, the more comfortable I become in my discomfort. In the words of Oprah 'what I know for sure' is that if I am not feeling some level of discomfort as I set my goals and take action, the goals just aren't big enough.

Writing this book also represents a type of liberation for me – I've wanted to write a book for a long time, but it seemed like such a BIG thing, that I just pushed it to the side. Fear is dangerous, because it can hold us back from stepping into our purpose, and it is only in stepping into our purpose that we find true joy. It's time for you (and me) to stop pushing our calling, and whatever steps and actions can fuel that calling, aside because of fear.

Chapter 2

The Courage to Ask
for what you want

This morning as I listened to a sermon by Bishop TD Jakes, one question resonated deeply with me – do you have the courage to ask? It takes courage to ask, to desire deeply and finally, to expect to receive. Too many of us don't ask for what we want out of fear of embarrassment or rejection, or based on the belief that our dreams are impossible and we won't get what we ask for. The truth is, because of some or all of those reasons, asking for what we want doesn't even occur to some of us. I shudder to think what I would not have achieved had I remained silent, what I would not have right now had I not had the courage to ask. You lose, over and over again, if you do not ask for what you want. Do you know how many times have you may have missed an opportunity simply because you did not speak up and ask?

The courage to ask demands self-belief. So, how do we develop self-belief? I think some of it has to do with mental conditioning. Since everything begins and ends in our minds, our highest priority must be conditioning our minds to understand that we are deserving of our dreams, and fully capable of manifesting them. Everything you see around you was once merely an idea, so why not you? Some of what has worked for me in this continuous, deliberate effort is prayer, visualization and vision boarding, reading, following, watching and absorbing advice, words, and examples of people who have achieved what I seek to, and practicing gratitude on a daily basis. I'm not sure why I used to be afraid to believe that I could achieve some of the grand dreams on my heart ... I am sure that psychologists have their own theories about the roots of our insecurities. I am not sure why it seems natural for us to limit ourselves. I know that when I wanted to start a business almost 8 years ago it was hard for me to imagine that I could run a successful business and I was very worried about being able to pay my bills at the end of the month without a guaranteed, steady paycheck. I couldn't imagine being responsible for the paychecks of another person! When I forced myself to write a bold 5 year goal it was to employ just two other people! Perhaps it was because I grew up with two parents, paid monthly and predictably, so I had no context for entrepreneurship? Maybe I am, by birth, risk averse? Whatever the reason, when I was inspired to start my own business, I was terrified. At some point though, after I practiced a combination of those things I listed above, daily, eventually I got it! Once I got that nothing truly separates me, at my very core, from others who have achieved their dreams and impacted the world in significant ways, an entire world opened up.

The mental conditioning required to get that everything I see around me in the world was once just an idea, executed by a human being with hopes and aspirations who were bold in their self-belief and unafraid to ask, and that nothing separates me from them other than a decision to practice a similar belief, is a conditioning that requires deliberate and daily effort. Each day, even as my business continues to grow, I must observe my thoughts closely, and challenge myself daily, to truly believe that I can build a global enterprise. What I have found to be extremely useful here is the identification of role models. When we can identify someone who has done what we seek to do, and learn how they did it, the many failures they worked through on their way to success, it shows us that it is all possible.

Once we believe that we deserve our highest dreams, and can achieve them, it is up to us to ask of God, of the Universe, of ourselves, and of others for whatever we need to fuel our dreams. I'm not talking about asking for handouts or waiting for others to give us what we need, I'm talking about bold faith, the kind that empowered me to call a prominent high school Principal and ask for permission to make a presentation to students at his school, even though I had no proven track record to speak of. Sure, I was afraid to hear no. The courage to ask means that we know that sometimes the answer will be no, but we are not afraid to hear 'no' secure in our knowledge that we will achieve our dreams, by one means or another. Plus, what do you really lose when you hear no? Nothing, because you didn't start out having that which you requested. Some Principals said no when I asked, but some said yes, and I built the foundation of my business on the yeses, and soon revisited the no's and turned them into yeses! What I know for sure, as Oprah would say, is that when you don't ask for what you want, you surrender control to others who may or may not feel like giving you want you want (if they even know that you want it!). So, what you don't ask for, you likely won't get. Is your pride or your fear more important to you than fulfilling your highest dreams? Practicing bold faith will feel incredibly uncomfortable at first, you may curl your toes and cringe, your heart rate may accelerate and your voice may tremble, but do it. You owe it to yourself!

Chapter 3

Tuning Into Your Purpose

One of the central concerns of those of us who seek a meaning-ful life is the question of How Do I Discover my Passion? I seek to first distinguish between passions which can be interests, hobbies and things we enjoy doing or are fascinated by and purpose, the reason for which something exists. Passions can function as the tools we use to carry out our purpose, but purpose is deeper than passion. Purpose should be more or less unchangeable, and really speak to the core of what impact we hope to have in the world. If there were no limiting factors, what would you change about the world? What do you want to accomplish or be remembered for?

TD Jakes said, "If you can't figure out your purpose, figure out your passion. For your passion will lead you right into your purpose".

How do you figure out your passion? Oprah wisely says, "Passion is energy. Feel the power that comes from focusing on what excites you." So, be curious! Make time (because let's face it, there never really is time, so you have to carve it out!) to try things, spend time on hobbies and pursuits that may be outside of the 9-5. We may actually not have found things that truly interest us because we don't try out enough things! When was the last time you tried something new? Perhaps there isn't one big, specific passion that is out there waiting to be discovered – perhaps there are many separate things that you may derive fulfillment from on their own and together they set you on fire. Don't be discouraged because you can't think of how to turn it into a business and do it 24/7 right now. I do believe however that our passions and career should fuel our purpose at some point. We must remain on the look out for the opportunities to bring passion and career together more and more, but yet not be too anxious if that is not the current state of our lives. I believe in setting a vision and having the courage to take action when opportunities do present themselves - as they will. Life has a way of bringing us face to face with exactly what we need, and if we are open, present and ready, we get it.

For me, the quest to tap into my purpose, the reason I exist, continues to involve prayer and paying attention to the things I just love to do, the things that set me on fire and get me excited (like speaking and advising), and considering how those things can be used in the service of my family, friends, community and the world. Tuning into my purpose has meant taking risks, and not being afraid to find myself not enjoying what I thought I would have. It has meant understanding that becoming an entrepreneur would not mean an immediate use of my newly (and expensively) acquired Masters Degree and Post Graduate Certificate but deciding to start my business anyway. In other words, I have to be open to the fact that my original plan may not be the one I will stick to. So, I am always open to changing the course along the way if I discover that it does not feel good to me. Eventually, there should be less and less separation between career and purpose and I think this incredible possibility is one that is open to us all.

Chapter 4

Procrastination

Procrastination often called "the thief of dreams" is an issue so many struggle with, and is, to some extent anyway, human nature. According to Psychology Today, we tend to discount our future, versus some present and immediate gratification. Highly successful people have the ability to reflect on themselves to understand their habits – the good and bad. So let's do some reflection.

Why do you procrastinate?

I tend to procrastinate when I feel overwhelmed, and I tend to feel overwhelmed when the goals seems too big or I've done a poor job of setting priorities and organizing myself, and my time, accordingly. Or, I procrastinate on things that I don't really want to do. I think we all

Nicole McLaren Campbell

need to take stock of what it is we really want and decide on what we must do to get there.

What do I really want?

Sometimes we tell ourselves we want to do things, but deep down they just aren't important enough to command action. Still, these things weigh on our minds and spirits, and cause us to lose faith in ourselves when we don't get them done. To help you get some clarity, consider what you've been procrastinating on, and complete the exercise below:

Task	Why do I need to do this?	What will happen if I DON'T do this?

Once you're clear on the what, the why AND the cost of not doing what you need to, you must try to hold clear mental images of the outcomes and possibilities of ACTION and INACTION. You have to imagine vividly the COST of not getting your tasks done. For a high school student procrastinating on homework and studying this may mean failing an exam, which will result in lowered GPA, which could affect chances of college admission.

Break it Down

Your goals must be broken down into tasks, and sub tasks of those tasks. Achieving smaller, micro goals will give you the momentum necessary to sustain action. Small daily actions are harder to procrastinate on, and add up to the big goal.

Make A List

To combat lack of organization, which leads to procrastination, I use LISTS daily. Whenever I stop using lists, I start feeling crazy, emotional, overwhelmed and out of control. Usually when these feelings come on, I remember that I haven't seen my to-do list book in a few days. I try to organize each day so that at least 2 of my 4 big, important quarterly goals get some attention. This way I make progress toward the things that are REALLY important to me, using small amounts of time daily, rather than waiting for some miracle block of time, which let's face it may or may not EVER happen! I used to wonder how super busy people, with high demand full-time jobs and families find the time to write books, sit on boards and take on other projects.

Read a book!

Since I learned that there was no specific super-human "type" off –limits to me I decide to learn what highly successful people are doing to seemingly create more hours in the day. It really comes down to organization and discipline. "Eat That Frog" by Brian Tracy has been a great resource for me in terms of organization and beating procrastination, so I highly recommend it to EVERYONE from the highly organized to the completely disorganized because no matter where we are in life, we can always up-level. The book is so good that there is something in there for everyone!

Consult an Expert on an Unfamiliar Goal

I've learned the value of having outside help and support because sometimes the task or goal feels so big and unfamiliar to me, fear and anxiety takes hold and I feel literally paralyzed. When I am in that zone, I procrastinate i.e. I take no action toward my goal, and surprise surprise, it doesn't happen. High performers have a tendency to believe they can do it all, while others are afraid to ask for help and/or view it as a sign of weakness. I confess, I never believed in "coaching" but when a high performing mentor of mine, a person I look up to, mentioned that he had weekly meetings with a business coach I became intrigued. As soon as I opened my mind up to the possibility that perhaps I could improve my performance if I had a coach, two appeared. Having worked with them for just a few months, my results have been beyond what I could have imagined because I have a clearer sense of how I can accomplish the particular goal. With that roadmap, I can create sub tasks and start taking action. The truth is, the added accountability also helps even the most elite performer. No matter what level we are at, we can aim higher and use a little help getting there!

Chapter 5

Staying Motivated

There is a famous Zig Ziglar quote that captures exactly how I feel about motivation "People often say that motivation doesn't last. Well, neither does bathing – that's why we recommend it daily." Sure, some days, (before I even open my eyes) I don't feel like doing anything but, the fact remains, the frequency and level of your intrinsic motivation will determine the extent to which you achieve your goals. How do I stay motivated most of the time? It isn't something that happens by chance, it is something that requires deliberate effort, every day.

Create a Routine

I've developed a morning routine, based on my understanding of myself, and how my brain works (which I've learned from reading books written by experts). When I wake up in the morning I first pray, expressing gratitude for the people in my life, for goals accomplished and goals to be accomplished, for abundance present and abundance on its way. This puts me in a winning, positive mood. I envision that my day will be filled with great opportunities, and I thank God for them too. Then, I exercise. I go running or to the gym, or both. Exercise is a powerful stimulant for me; I literally feel the endorphins lifting my mood after I exercise. Getting up early in the morning and exercising discipline also makes me feel like a winner, like an elite performer doing what most people are unwilling to do. The next part of my morning routine involves sitting at my desk and writing a clear to-do-list with clear high priority and low priority goals for the day. Each week is guided by 3 or 4 overall important goals so each day I am clear that I must do something in the direction of those very important goals. Then, I ensure that I complete my first task which MUST be my least desired task since I know that my energy level and motivation is higher in the morning versus the afternoon or worse, the evening when all I want to do is head home and relax with my family.

When is your energy level naturally highest? Practicing a routine daily puts me in the driver's seat - as much as possible I try to happen to life as opposed to allowing it to happen to me. Do you have a morning routine?

Feeding My Mind

Another key aspect of staying motivated has to do with feeding my mind. For example, reading biographies and articles about successful people, following my role models on social media, this all shows me that they go through all kinds of problems, just like me, on their way to success. I am reminded that life happens to everyone – the good and the bad – and that there is no real reason why I can't achieve what it is I envision. Feeding your brain with empowering messages is a major key to staying motivated. What do you feed your mind? Your inner circle of friends will also exert a significant impact on your level of motivation, because whether you like it or not, you absorb their energy and mindset after continuous exposure, over time. This is a fact that I have experienced over and over in my own life. I rely on my friends to remind me of my greatness when I am feeling low and doubting my possibilities or myself. My friends challenge me and often push me beyond my comfort zone. I do the same for them. I remind them of who they are when they forget. It's taken a while for me but I am finally at peace with having a relatively small inner circle. Are your friends feeding your brain or draining your energy, most of the time?

Do What You Need to Do

For me, keeping my outer-self put together helps me stay powered up and feeling like a winner. I have determined that #FixUpFridays is a non-negotiable part of my schedule, a weekly appointment where I get my hair and nails done. I'm working on incorporating a monthly massage and facial - I am testing it out to see how that feels but overall, it is very important for me to feel put together so that I can power forward with full confidence.

Rest When You Need To

Staying motivated also requires you to pace yourself and get adequate rest. I have really, really struggled with this because of a false association I made with working all the time and success. With the help of my husband and sisters, I am getting better at understanding how to balance my energy, pull back when I need to, and build time for rest and relaxation into my schedule. When I start to approach burn out and exhaustion I feel completely de-motivated and it takes a few days (sometimes longer) for me to get back to my baseline level of motivation. Do you know when you need to take a break? Can you discipline yourself to do so?

It's All Connected

As you may have noticed, many of the themes are connected. For example, many struggle with staying motivated (and procrastination) because they haven't tuned in to their purpose by spending time on their passions (doing what they enjoy, or what excites them). Without the ability to move beyond fear and practice self-belief and the courage to ask for what you want, it is impossible to fully pursue one's purpose. It is difficult to stay motived if we feel confused about where we are headed, or overwhelmed by too many things with no clear sense of direction. Without some sense of purpose and overall vision for one's life, it is hard to become, and stay motivated. So, it is indeed all connected.

Chapter 6

Bonus: InstaFriends' Questions

Q: *How does one know his true passion(s)?*
A: I believe that knowing one's passion is a process of discovery that
comes out of trying different things, based on curiosity, an inkling,
a gut feeling ... and perhaps piecing those things together and pursuing them so as to deepen that interest, over time. People make
the mistake of thinking that if it's your purpose, you will love everything involved in pursuing it, everyday. I have found that to be
very far from true - I believe I am tuning in to my purpose - empowering people - however some parts of the pursuit feel onerous,
but it doesn't make empowerment any less of my purpose. I have a
passion for speaking, and it is one of the ways I fulfill my purpose.
As I wrote about in Chapter 3, if you are pursuing your passion(s)

it should give you energy and excitement. I know that I am pursuing my passions when I feel most alive.

Q: *How do you deal with consistent disappointments?*

A: No one likes being disappointed! However, setbacks are a necessary part of success - don't believe me? Read the life story of any successful person you respect, and during that journey you will inevitably find failure, setbacks and disappointments of varying scales. So, first I remind myself that as cliche as it may sound "failure is a part of success" and I replay the failures of people I know, or know of, who are successful. Depending on the size of the disappointment I may give myself a set time to mourn / indulge in a pity party, then I discipline myself to focus my energy and attention on possible solutions if the disappointment has created an issue that needs to be addressed. Even if the problem seems to have no possible bright side, I challenge myself to find one or to find a lesson to be learned that I can apply to a future situation. If I've found a solution or opportunity in the setback or failure, I pursue it immediately. If I haven't found a solution or opportunity, and the situation is absolutely and entirely out of my control, I move on to tackle another issue or focus on another unrelated area or opportunity. I try NOT to take disappointments personally (again, reminding myself that failure is a necessary part of success), and continue to be driven by a firm belief in self.

Q: *How do you recognize your talents to better maximize your potential?*

A: I recognized my talents mostly because other people recognized them in me, and brought them to my attention. However, in areas where I am not naturally talented that are important in some way to my development, I try to learn as much as possible until I become skilled. Lisa Nichols once told me that what is one persons natural talent is another's learned skill-set. So, once you outline your vision for your life, you then look at what skills are necessary to achieve the goals fueling the vision, then either learn them yourself, or else partner with or hire someone who can apply them.

Q: *How do you change directions in your life when you want to be your own boss, but you don't know how to get started?*

A: Successfully changing directions and venturing into entrepreneurship requires clarity around your vision, a plan with as much research and detail as possible supported by goals with a timeline and a few other things ... but in the end you are going to need bold self-belief and courage to take the first step, and the self-discipline to keep stepping, every day.

Q: *How do you perfect your resume and ace interviews?*

A: One thing I love about being alive in 2017 is the accessibility of information - we are a click away from most things we hope to learn - including creating a compelling resume and acing interviews. There is a wealth of information available online, but my tips are to create a resume that is concise (no longer than 1 page) and reflects your deep knowledge of what your potential employer's highest needs are. You should use active language to articulate how your prior experience has equipped you with the skills necessary to meet (and exceed) your potential employer's needs and expectations.

Q: *How do you attain your goals when you have drive and determination but minimal resources?*

A: Focus on what you do have, and take the first step. If you do the research, you will find that many people started out with even less than you have and found a way to accomplish their dream. You might need to start with a smaller goal and build up to that big goal.

Q: *How do I come out of my comfort zone?*

A: Nothing significant happens in one's comfort zone! So, you really have to get clear about just how badly you want what it is you say you want for your life - and take the leap! Then do it again. And again. And again. Getting out of your comfort zone requires the development then consistent flexing of self-discipline - and it gets easier with practice!

Q: *With a 9-5 that is very demanding how do I start my business in 2017 without leaving my job?*

A: Let me share a very good piece of advice from Lisa Nichols and repeated in different words by Thione Niang - save, save, save all you possibly can making every sacrifice humanly possible, while working, to fund your dream of leaving your current 9-5 to start your business. There is no nobility in not being able to pay your bills and take care of your responsibilities due to lack of planning around becoming an entrepreneur.

Q: *How do you know for sure that you have chosen the best career path / business suited for you?*

A: I experience deep satisfaction, pride and a feeling of joy from the impact I am able to have on the lives of people - young and old - in terms of empowering them to achieve their dreams. It is in direct line with my vision and mission. But, I am open to manifesting this vision in various capacities. So, I think that you should remain open to exploring different paths as long as they are all in line with your vision - what you want to do in the world and the type of impact you want to have.

Q: *What are the ways to create balance, especially under pressure?*

A: I feel as though I am under pressure, all the time, unless I force myself to take a break! Even right now as I type I am under pressure. So - I breathe and pray, every morning first thing, plus during the course of the day. I follow the routine I outlined in Chapter 5 every day. I also try to be as organized as possible, and schedule everything - including family time and me time. If you don't run your life, your life runs you, so remain in control by having an organized schedule and systems in place.

Q: *How do you stay motivated when you have reached a plateau?*

A: When I have reached a plateau I know its time to do something differently. I may need to read a new book, take a mental break and watch junk TV for a bit, sleep, or travel to a conference to refuel and expose myself to visionaries and high energy inspiration folks to remind me of who I am, and what I am capable of.

Q: *Does one have to follow one pursuit / passion or can one have multiple? If so what are the best ways to streamline and still be effective and achieve maximum results?*

A: I read something powerful in Grit by Angela Duckworth and it was an exercise that Warren Buffett gave to his pilot which involved writing down 25 career / life goals then choosing the 5 most important ones, and deciding to cross out and ignore the other 20 at all costs! The rationale was that the other 20 will distract your focus from the top 5. When I heard that I was terrified since I like to think that I am open to pursuing many paths - but the truth is that we do have finite personal resources in terms of time, and it takes time to become really good at something and therefore excel in it. So, just don't go down too many disconnected roads if you hope to have a great impact.

Q: *What intentions did you set out for yourself when you became a blogger?*

A: I really didn't set any, formally anyway. I just want to share my experience with the hope that it can help someone.

Conclusion

My mission is to inspire as many people as I can, to help awaken them to the vast possibilities that life, and their own lives, hold. Books have helped me so much, in so many ways, that I can't imagine being true to my mission and NOT writing books. Thank you for giving me the opportunity to share some tips on how, driven by "unrealistic" expectations, I'm moving beyond my fear daily, to create the life I want to live. I hope you will now (continue) to do the same. AIM Higher!

About the Author

Nicole Campbell is an educator, entrepreneur and professional speaker. Driven by a passion for empowerment, she represented Jamaica at MIT's Junior Summit and was selected to address then UN Secretary General Kofi Annan at just 13 years old. She was subsequently featured in local and international media, including CNN and Nickelodeon and was chosen as one of "20 Teens Who Will Change the World" by Teen People Magazine.

She is a graduate of the St. Andrew High School for Girls in Jamaica, Phillips Academy 'Andover' in Massachusetts and Princeton University. Nicole also studied at Stanford University's Summer Institute and the University of London, where she earned a Masters Degree in Globalization and Development.

Nicole returned to Jamaica immediately upon completion of her Masters degree to join the Ministry of Education where she served as Senior Policy Analyst to the then Minister of Education, now Prime Minister of Jamaica, the Most Hon. Andrew Holness. At 25, Nicole resigned from the Ministry to start AIM Educational Services – with just two students. Nicole sites her decision to tap into her passion for human development in education as one of the best she's made. Today, AIM sees hundreds of students and delivers an average return of over 5000% to parents – results Nicole attributes to a strong, motivated team whose focus remains on possibilities, not problems. She recently started the AIM Higher Foundation with a mandate to identify, develop and empower promising low-income students so that they too can access unlock their potential through access to tertiary education.

Parents seek Nicole for the impact she has on their teenagers – how she pushes them to adopt empowering perspectives and to create possibilities for their futures, with their present actions. Her passion for empowerment extends beyond the classroom to the boardroom and beyond. Noted for her no-nonsense, yet practical approach, Nicole addresses corporate and public audiences on the subject of maximizing potential in their personal and professional lives. Each year she speaks to thousands of teenagers at high schools across Jamaica and addresses corporate audiences on the subject of maximizing one's potential. She also serves as a Board Member of the Early Childhood Commission and the CHASE Fund in Jamaica, and is a Career & Education Columnist for the Jamaica Observer focusing on College Preparation. In her own words, "everything that I do is really an extension of my passion to empower people – to me, nothing can match the excitement and sense of fulfillment I get from helping people to grow in confidence and realize their potential."

She is wife to reggae artiste Assassin aka Agent Sasco (Jeffrey Campbell), mom to 5-year old LC, 4-year-old Joshua and 'bonus-mom' to 11-year-old Ally. She loves taking videos of her kids and posting them to her favourite social media platform: Instagram. A self-professed inspirational quote junkie, her personal motto is "AIM High and Be Bold" and her mission is to squeeze every ounce of life, from life.

NICOLE MCLAREN CAMPBELL
is available for readings, lectures and speaking engagements.
To inquire about an appearance, please contact
info@nicolemclarencampbell.com

Made in the USA
Middletown, DE
27 March 2019